The Indivisible Body of Reality

POEMS

Teresa Mei Chuc

The Indivisible Body of Reality

Copyright © 2025 by Teresa Mei Chuc

All rights reserved. No part of this book may be reproduced or transmitted in any form or by any means without written permission of the author.

Cover Art: "Our Grandkids Can Only See The Animals On TV"
by Ann Phong

ISBN 9781737711384

Library of Congress Control Number: 2025941923

Published by Shabda Press
Duarte, California
www.shabdapress.com

"Contemplation on interdependence is a deep looking into all phenomena in order to pierce through to their real nature, in order to see them as part of the great body of reality, and in order to see that the great body of reality is indivisible. It cannot be cut into pieces that exist separately from each other." —Thích Nhất Hạnh

Contents

Mother of Water, River of Nine Dragons 1
Rescued Tigers 3
Saola 4
Hoang Lien Son Mountains 5
My Mother is a River 7
Monsoon 9
The Two-Headed Fish 10
cuống rốn 11
Praying at the Whale Temple in Vũng Tàu 12
When rubber trees replace native rainforests 13
After the American War 14
Salted Fish 16
Moon Bear 17
Sonnet for a Mountain Lion 18
What the U.S. Calls Counter-Terrorism: 19
Yellow Power 20
Lesson in Geometry and
the Redistribution of Resources 22
Hoy Sum 23
Electrocardiogram 24
Moon Song 25

97 degrees fahrenheit outside 26
Ace of Spades 27
The most blood I remember seeing 28
Mach 1 29
Tres Hermanas 30
My Sadness is as Great
as a Mountain: A Haibun 31
Fire / Earth / Metal / Water / Wood 32
We are the leaves. 34
Poem to Los Angeles 35
Sonnet for the People 36
Famine 38
Acknowledgments 41

for my family, my ancestors and Mother Earth

Mother of Water, River of Nine Dragons

"Dam construction on the Mekong River poses a serious threat to the region's economies and ecosystems. The only way to mitigate that threat is to end defiant unilateralism and embrace institutionalized collaboration focused on protecting each country's rights and enforcing its obligations – to its people, its neighbors, and the planet." – Brahma Chellaney (August 2, 2019)

Sông Mê Kông, flowing from the Tibetan Plateau
through China, Myanmar,
Laos, Thailand, Cambodia, Vietnam
and into the country of my heart

where the wild rice grows
and the villagers live and have lived
for thousands of years,

where the Irrawaddy dolphins,
the giant catfish and the softshell turtles swim,

where the sarus cranes feed
on insects, seeds, fish in the river reeds,
and open their majestic wings to take flight,

where the lilies and lotus bloom,
where our ancestors are alive,

where the water buffalo bathe
their thousand-pound body
submerged in the river of my soul
their heads on the water's surface
curving horns pointing towards the sky,

where Sông Cửu Long,
River of Nine Dragons flow
through thick palm and green mangrove forests
where the douc langur and white-cheeked gibbon exist,

and the salt and fresh water mix,

I, your daughter, am forever connected to you
though thousands of miles away.

Rescued Tigers

"In 2016, the World Wide Fund for Nature estimated that fewer than five tigers remain in Vietnam's forests."

The seven rescued indochinese baby tiger cubs are so cute.
I look into their eyes and see the gray blue sky and our own resilience.

How many more *lasts* will I experience in my lifetime?
In 2009, the last wild rhinoceros was shot and killed by poachers in Vietnam.

Our rainforests are pillaged.
The eyes of the tiger cubs are the sky.

I am afraid when they will close forever,
because we need each other.

Saola

You come to me in dreams
from my Motherland
emerging from the forest
your horns like black swords

How many wars have you survived?

How I try to live like you
evading hunters that are
always in search of me.

Hoang Lien Son Mountains

Uncle pointed at the mountain range
in the distance. He said, "Hoang Lien Son Mountains."
It was so green and beautiful like an emerald.

I heard of that name before, from my father.
Hoang Lien Son Mountains was where he was
imprisoned in a Viet Cong "re-education" camp for nine years.

But this poem is not about the prison camp
or the suffering of my father and the other prisoners
—that is another poem.

In these mountains are critically endangered
western black crested gibbons who live and eat
in the trees, swinging from branch to branch.

The gibbons talk to each other in a language
that my father listened to for nearly a decade.
At dawn, swinging in the trees,
a chorus of howls,
birdlike chirps and whistles.
While hanging from a branch,
a gibbon reaches her hand to scoop up
water from a stream and drinks.

These mountains are a sacred home
to the few remaining species of gibbons,
primates like us.

As when I visited Con Son Island,
I wondered why there is so much pain
in a beautiful place. How much could
humans take without giving back?

My Mother is a River

Mekong Delta, Việt Nam

nước nước nước
nước
nước
nước

is the sound of our survival

In Vietnamese, the word for
"water" means "country."
We are a country of water,
where thousands of rivers flow
like the arteries and veins in my body.
We are a people of water—
we plant and harvest rice,
ride canoes and sampans,
walk knee deep in water, swim,
catch fish with our bare hands
and handmade nets.

We are a people who, at dawn,
ride bamboo boats
out to gather morning dew
from lotus petals.

We walk barefoot through life,
our toes and legs dig into mud.

Sông Mê Kông delta soil,
water, imprinted into my DNA.

There are now cracks in the river
bottom with crevices
like the geography of a brain.
The delta is drying out where rice
grew plentifully for thousands of years.

My mother once told me, "As long as
you have rice, you will survive."

What will villagers do now?
The numerous dams upstream
causing floods and disrupting
the river's flow.
Where will the fish go?
What is happening to the endangered
river dolphin, the giant catfish,
the softshell turtle?

Where would mặt trăng,
moon, see her own reflection?

Monsoon

People who live in regions
of monsoons know that everything
you build is transitory

Palm and bamboo huts on stilts
could be washed away
and broken by a wave

So they build knowing
how many times they must rebuild

The Two-Headed Fish

that the poor Vietnamese family
eats or they will starve,

haunts me.
It floats in the air
like some kind of monster
in the night while I sleep.

Decades after the war,
Agent Orange
is still transforming
the genetics of the fish
in our rivers.

cuống rốn

my mother says
that my umbilical cord
was given to the land

buried in Việt Nam
part of me a part of the earth
there forever

perhaps giving birth to hoa sứ

                champa flowers

Praying at the Whale Temple in Vũng Tàu

"A person who spots a dead whale [in the village] has the responsibility to mourn the death with all the rituals carried out when his/her parent or grandparent passes away." - On Vietnam's southern coast, a cemetery for whales by Truong Ha

At the whale temple,
I kneel down to pray
to the bones of the sea gods
on the altar who bear many names—
Cá Ông, Grandfather fish,
cá voi, elephant fish,
made from a robe and elephant bones
tossed into the sea by Quan Âm Bồ Tát.
I offer incense and flowers
to our great ancestors
who watch over us in the sea,
who have saved many fishermen
in storms, who have balanced boats
and people on their backs.

The fishermen and villagers
bring a beached whale
to the land where she is
given a funeral procession.

There is a whale cemetery
in Bà Rịa - Vũng Tàu Province
in the fishing village
of Phước Hải
where hundreds of whales
are buried, incense and flowers
on each grave.

A woman kneels and prays.

When rubber trees replace native rainforests

for monoculture farming to grow a cash crop
where indigenous trees, medicinal plants, gold snub-nosed

monkeys, elephants, tigers, deer, rivers, lakes, folk songs, dances
thrived. Ancestors buried on hills live with gods in sacred forests

we don't enter or remove even a leaf, because everything
there has a purpose in the whole ecosystem.

In another world, holding a cell phone with its rubber case,
watching car tires roll by on busy streets,

wherever we turn, we touch rubber.
It is somewhere in our room, in our bodies.

What was taken away to live like this?

After the American War

and after spending nine years
in a Vietcong reeducation camp
away from his family,
my father plants cilantro, coriander
ngò, ngò rí, rau mùi, rau răm,
Thai basil, húng quế, lemongrass, xả,
perilla, tía tô.

He plants guava trees, grapefruit trees,
dragon fruits that climb a delicate trellis he's built
with old furniture, the fruit a fluorescent pink.

My father's passion fruit vines cover my old
bedframe, from my bed when I was a child,
the frame raised above the ground
on the four corners, so that I could crawl
under and be surrounded by passion fruit and
magical blossoms.

My father's longan tree is full of sweet perfumed fruits
that the neighborhood birds and I long for.
Plants and trees from our Vietnamese homeland
fill bố mẹ's garden in East Pasadena.

My father is healing from the American war,
his hands holding the earth, his hands holding
a branch he cut from which he will grow into a new tree.

This is the side of my father I want to remember
and not the one who threw a knife at me when I was a child
for using my left hand to write, not the one who chased me
with an ax saying he was going to kill me, not the one overcome
with trauma and loss of homeland and being separated from
his family, not the father who endured prison for nine years
not knowing if he would ever be released and see his family again,
the one boiling with anger.

My father picks the guavas from his garden for us to eat.
Each fruit is delicious and grown with care.
My father has never told me that he loves me,
but he gathers the Vietnamese herbs he grew
for the homemade phở he spent two days cooking for us.

Salted Fish

The memory of my grandmother
hanging fish to dry in the warm California sun
shortly after we, refugees, arrived in this country.

Sun dried fish were one of my favorite foods
to eat with plain, steaming rice.

The smell was strong and filled
the air in the garden with the scent

of our Mother Ocean connecting
us to our Vietnamese homeland.

Salted, dried sunfish and perch—
my grandmother's love keeps us alive.

Moon Bear

crescent moon
luminous on your chest

sacred bear of our rainforests
your fur is the night sky

Quan Âm's emissary of compassion
so near extinction due to illegal

bile farming and deforestation
metal traps set by poachers

I can not imagine you
living out your life in a small cage

to be exploited, your bile extracted
from gallbladder through a tube

moon bear, our relative
and ancestor

in my dream, we stand
under the moonlight

side by side
in the forested hills
of our homeland

Sonnet for a Mountain Lion

We made you into some kind of Hollywood Star
Trapped on an island surrounded by freeways
You crossed a treacherous path of speeding cars
And for years were here to stay

Alone without rivals or mates
In the limelight you shine
In this establishment – your fate
Next to the Hollywood sign

People let you live as long as they feel safe in their hillside houses
As long as you are not perceived as a threat
On this land that is yours before anyone else's
We need you, this balance of life and should never forget

People attempt to make you theirs, name you P-22
Collar and track you but to the land you will always be true

What the U.S. Calls Counter-Terrorism:

The Phoenix Program

Not only did the U.S.
try to steal our native land,
it tried to steal our firebird

Embroidered it onto
patches and gave
those who wore
it a job to assassinate

Calling anyone they believed
to be an insurgent
or Viet Cong or
protecting their own
homeland, a terrorist.

Yellow Power

after Amy Uyematsu

In middle school, I would look in the mirror
and tell myself, "I am beautiful." Over and over again.
Even though, looking at billboards,
magazines and T.V., I thought that I was not.

My nose is the right size, I am the right height,
My black hair is the right color,
My brown eyes are beautiful. My skin is the right color.
There is nothing *wrong* with me.

When my tongue stumbles over English words
and grammar it's because I already
hold two native languages within me—
carried across the ocean in our refugee boat,

Vietnamese and Cantonese.

It's okay if I do not hold a knife,
fork and spoon the "correct" way,
they aren't my utensils of choice.
Chopsticks were my first utensils;

I could use them to do a thousand things—
pick up rice grains one by one, cut noodles,
hold up my hair in a bun.

My school lunch sometimes smells of fish sauce,
nước mắm. Some kids ask what that stinky smell is.
A sauce from my Vietnamese Motherland,
so loved by my family and people.

I, too, refuse to feel shame and exclaim myself–I am nước mắm,
delicious and proud…scent and taste that will remain.

Lesson in Geometry and the Redistribution of Resources

When I was little, for years, Mother would bring home brown paper towels she took from the restroom at work.

I remember folding and unfolding them with my small hands. Three equal parts forward and backward.

I didn't understand that we were poor but I could smell it in the scent of the paper and feel it in the roughness against my face.

I learned a lesson in yin and yang before I even knew what it meant.

I did not feel shame but only love as I imagined my mother quickly pulling paper after paper after paper from the metal dispenser in the restroom and hiding them in her purse to bring home to my brother and me.

Hoy Sum

In Cantonese, the word for "happiness" is "hoy sum"
"hoy" means "open" and "sum" means "heart"
"happiness" is "open heart"
drumming a hundred thousand beats a day
happiness - thousands of orange poppies in bloom,
lighting up the hillside and soaking in the spring sun
with their hearts wide open.

Electrocardiogram

In Vietnamese, to live, "sống,"
is a river, "dòng sông,"
and ocean waves, "sóng biển"

"To live" carries within it
river and ocean waves.

Mother said to me when
I was a little girl and learning
what it means to live,
"Life is like the ocean,
sometimes the waves
are so strong it could topple
your boat and sometimes
the waves are calm."

My heart makes a picture
of waves. This is how
she moves through life.

Moon Song

It took me decades
to realize that this blood
is a song of life

and not a lament

droplets on my skirt

droplets on my bed sheets,
my underwear when I wake

so many small red moons
dipped in the reddest
of ink, my blood
refuse to be washed away

my blood singing
songs of my ancestors
mothers, grandmothers
through each cotton fiber
reminding me

my body is giver of life
and this blood is the most
beautiful red

97 degrees fahrenheit outside

A person lays on concrete in the rectangular
shade of a building's awning.
Wearing a jacket, their only clothing.
Motionless but alive.
In the sun, the pavement is 145 degrees.

Wearing a jacket, their only clothing.
Cars pass by. People walk by.
In the sun, the pavement is 145 degrees.
There is a loneliness in the body that wraps
itself up in front of a shop.

Cars pass by. People walk by.
Motionless but alive.
There is a loneliness in the body that wraps
itself up in front of a shop.
A person lays on concrete in the rectangular
shade of a building's awning.

Ace of Spades

Việt Nam War

There were 1,000 Ace of Spades cards pulled from the production line by the U.S. card company and shipped overseas at no cost for American soldiers to use.

Decks of pure 52 Ace of Spades cards were produced. A Death Deck. Mothers sent them to their sons.

An Ace of Spades card was left on the forehead of a Vietnamese person killed. U.S. military tactic to instill fear in the people fighting to defend their homeland.

Supported by the U.S. corporate machine, supported by tax dollars.

The most blood I remember seeing

was when I gave birth to my son.
The blood covered his small body and
dribbled out of mine. And then the doctor
pulled the placenta out from within me.
It was covered with my blood. I had never
seen so much of my blood outside of my body.
Itself creating another human being and somehow
this brought me great joy and also great fear.
It must be the first step to losing and parting.
This must be the greatest fear in my first
experience of separating from something
that was such a part of me that my cells themselves
created him.

I remember seeing so much blood when I watched
the news and the Palestinian child running among
rubble after bombings was covered in blood
and I wondered if it was the blood of his mother.

Mach 1

    a bullet

sonic boom

the speed of sound is about 760 miles per hours

the speed of a bullet is slower than the time it takes to love

Tres Hermanas

After the 2024 Presidential election, I started a school garden in L.A. and taught my students about seeds. My 6th & 7th graders choose seeds they want to plant on the first day our garden club meets.

They scoop soil into small pots and plant their seeds. I teach my students they could take something so small so freely given by the earth and grow something that will sustain them.

I teach my students to touch the earth with their hands and that the return to the earth is power for them, their families and their communities. I teach them to nurture, to water the pots where they planted seeds.

I teach them how we need sunlight and rain. Two weeks later, every seed planted by every student – snap peas, radish, brussel sprouts, blue corn, honey melon sprout into seedlings in the greenhouse.

I teach my students that the future is still theirs. They plant their future working together with the earth and each other. Before winter break,

we plant the corn plants grown from seeds, now three inches tall, into a growing bed, put beans into the soil next to the corn. Propagate squash in small pots. My students learn about the tres hermanas.

How we grow them together and how they help each other to survive like us.

My Sadness is as Great as a Mountain: A Haibun

I was a two-year-old child lost in the seas of the aftermath of war; my family and I, Vietnamese boat refugees, who started a new life in Pasadena. Growing up in the City of Roses, I attended Hamilton Elementary and Marshall Fundamental Jr./Sr. High School and soon found my second home in the stones and stream that flowed through Eaton Canyon, where I learned to balance, jumping from rock to rock up the stream to the waterfall. In these mountains, I learned to fall and to get up again. Learned that sometimes climbing down was more difficult than climbing up, because gravity could make you slip. The oak trees and bay laurels wrapped their arms around my sadness and I felt loved. The deer taught me about the possibilities of life. The canyon gave me a silence that I could not find at home. The bird chirps offered me hope and joy, a counter to my father's PTSD and rage after fighting in the Vietnam War and spending nine years in a Vietcong prison. My family and I lost our Vietnamese Motherland and so much more. In these mountains, I found my other home. When the fires burned in Altadena in the New Year of 2025, my mountain burned down. The trees, trails and streams that offered me friendship, that strengthened my body, mind and spirit, not only in childhood but throughout my life, were engulfed in flames, as was my heart. Black bears, squirrels, deer ran frantically. The wings of birds caught on fire and the fur of coyotes burned. Many friends lost their homes and many had to evacuate as the fire raced down the mountain. But I know, in time, the mountain will return again and so will we. Life, like pine cones opening to release seeds after a fire, will grow from the ashes. Indian paintbrush, mariposa lily, native chia, black sage– fire-followers.

<blockquote>
my heart
the Santa Ana winds today
branches fall to the ground
</blockquote>

Fire / Earth / Metal / Water / Wood

Fire

Spring is here
the California poppies bloom
lit like candles along the streets
the petals glow and warm me like a fire
I'm with an old friend
bright orange and smiling
I bend down and say hello

Earth

We wear a nón lá on our head
a mountain made of palm leaves sewn
over round strips of bamboo bent into concentric circle frames
the way circles form when a pebble drops into a pond

We wear the earth on our head, the plants of our Motherland.
Along the rice fields, people are bent over in the hot sun,
each carrying a mountain on their head and in the distance, another mountain.

Metal

I hold my Tai chi sword balancing on one leg
looking at my target ready to strike the way sarus cranes
catch a fish with their long beaks in the Mekong river,
the way my ancestors have held a sword for thousands of years
defending their lives, families and homeland from invaders.

What is this talk about passive, quiet Asian women?
See how the metal flickers in the sunlight and the wings of a crane open.

Water

"Nước," the word for water, in Vietnamese is also the word for "country" or "homeland"

I am in the river in a basket boat,
the water is as green as the surrounding mangrove trees.
The gibbons are singing to each other as they hang from the branches.
I think of the poet who said that time is a river and we are the river.
I am floating in time, in a river, in myself and I am time.

Wood

We gather branches from the tree of music, the native elderberry, surrounded by the fragrant blossoms that will turn into delicious berries this summer. I planted this tree almost ten years ago, and now it is taller than me. We saw a long, straight branch into sections for three clapper sticks, choose our part of the branch, peel the bark and using a small axe, we split three quarters of the stick and hollow out the soft pith. Our friend plays a playlist from Tony Cerda and indigenous songs as we test out our clapper sticks, tapping the split branches against our palm. Suddenly, the heart of the earth is beating, and I feel it synchronize with my heartbeat.

We are the leaves

(Summer 2025, resistance against ICE raids)

that fall from the sycamore
the wind that caresses
the earth that receives
the rain that nurtures
the fire that burns
and melts the icy hand of tyranny
in our city

Poem to Los Angeles

(Summer 2025 ICE raids and U.S. military occupation)

after Marina Tsvetaeva

They took   quickly, they took   forcefully,
   took the street vendor and the day laborer.
They took our mother, and took our brother
   from us, aunties they took also and neighbors.

They took the farmworker, and they took the strawberry picker.
   They took the PhD student and took the professor.
They took the patient, and took the nurse
   they took the books from us, and took the words.

Diversity   they took and equity   they took.
   They took family and friends.
But   worse than taking home on earth from us
   they won the battle for our spirits and minds.

Food they took from us, they took our water
   clean air they took, and freedom too.
But while we continue to care for and protect each other
   the whole city   is still armed.

Sonnet for the People

June 25, 2025

My mother told me when the Vietnamese
government took Father away at the
Fall of Saigon, she was pregnant with me.
Father fought in the Southern army that

was under the United States' control.
Their strategy - divide and conquer us.
We fled Vietnam in a refugee boat.
In Heaven and the sea, we put our trust.

My father was imprisoned for nine years.
Now flash forward, terror and ICE raids in
our neighborhoods throughout Los Angeles,
street vendors selling flowers, fruits being

kidnapped by masked, armed men in unmarked cars,
day laborers snatched from the Home Depot
parking lots. National Guard troops at war
with people they should protect. All for show.

This is not new, fascist, U.S. Empire,
the state and the treatment of the people.
Protest in peace while LAPD fires.
On stolen land, no one is illegal.

Neighbors taken away in handcuffs while
Gaza is bombed and the people starved
using our tax dollars, dead bodies pile.
Genocide in history's stone being carved.

Before our eyes as we scroll, babies die.
The concrete of a building that was bombed,
body parts scattered as we live a lie.
Everything depends on how we respond.

U.S. marines deployed to L.A. streets.
The government threatened by how much we
take care of one another, our drum beats.
We, the people, have the power TO BE.

Here, in L.A., in Vietnam, in Gaza
'round the world, "Solo el pueblo, salva

al pueblo."

Famine

We plant starters in our plot
at the community garden—
kale
lettuce
serrano pepper
jalapeño pepper
zucchini
tomatillo
tomato
eggplant
cilantro
basil
pole bean
bitter melon

I am grateful we could grow
our own food
but am saddened that the Palestinian
people are starving and can not
grow food in their own homeland.

I look at pictures of Vietnamese children
during the Great Famine from 1944 to 1945–
Nạn đói Ất Dậu

when 1 to 2 million Vietnamese people
died of starvation.

I see their rib cages and bones wrapped in skin
so thin like the children, babies and people of Gaza now.

I wonder how the world responded when my ancestors were dying of starvation during the Japanese occupation of French Indochina.

Did the world feel our pain and empty bellies deprived of food in our own homeland that grows so abundantly?

Acknowledgments

"97 degrees fahrenheit outside" - *sin cesar*, 2024
"Ace of Spades" - *Cultural Daily*, Summer 2023
"After the American War" - 2025 Câylendar, a project run by Đùm Bọc
"cuống rốn" - *Cultural Daily*, Summer 2023
"Electrocardiogram" - *Rosebud Literary Magazine*, 2025
"Hoang Lien Son Mountains" - *Here Was Once the Sea: An Anthology of Southeast Asian Ecowriting* (University of Hawaii Press, 2024)
"Monsoon" - *Cultural Daily*, Summer 2023
"Mother of Water, River of Nine Dragons" - *The Tiger Moth Review*, 2020, *Colossus: Current* (Colossus Press, 2025)
"My Mother is a River" - *Here Was Once the Sea: An Anthology of Southeast Asian Ecowriting* (University of Hawaii Press, 2024)
"My Sadness is as Great as a Mountain: A Haibun" - *Altadena Poetry Review 2025* (online), *Altadena Poetry Review 2026* (print version)
"Poem to Los Angeles" - *About Place Journal*, Volume VIII, Issue IV, "On Freedom" (2025) and *Fortieth Anniversary Veterans for Peace 2025 National Convention*
"Praying at the Whale Temple in Vũng Tàu" - *Incidental Takes* (Hummingbird Press, 2023)
"Rescued Tigers" - *The Global South Journal*, Fall 2022
"Salted Fish" - *Along the Way, We Saw the World: A 20th Anniversary Collection of Prose and Poetry* (826LA, 2025)
"Saola" - *Here Was Once the Sea: An Anthology of Southeast Asian Ecowriting* (University of Hawaii Press, 2024), *Little Things: An Anthology of Poetry* (Ethos Books, 2025)
"Sonnet for a Mountain Lion" - *Artemis Journal*, 2023
"Sonnet for the People" - *Peace & Planet News*, Summer 2025
"The most blood I remember seeing" - *How One Loses Notes and Sounds* (Word Palace Press, 2016)
"The Two-Headed Fish" - *Cultural Daily*, Summer 2023
"Tres Hermanas" - *Anger is a Gift: Anthology of Resistance and Response Poems to the 2024 Election* (FlowerSong Press, 2025)
"What the U.S. Calls Counter-Terrorism: The Phoenix Program" - *The Night Heron Barks*, Fall 2020
"When rubber trees replace native rainforests" – Terrain.org, July 5, 2023
"Yellow Power" - https://discovernikkei.org/en/ and *Altadena Poetry Review: Anthology 2024* (Golden Foothills Press, 2024)

www.ingramcontent.com/pod-product-compliance
Lightning Source LLC
Chambersburg PA
CBHW051704040426
42446CB00009B/1298